D1486692

Women in Science

BY SUE BRADFORD EDWARDS

CONTENT CONSULTANT
Diana B. Erchick, PhD
Professor, Mathematics Education, K–12
The Ohio State University, Newark

Essential Library
An Imprint of Abdo Publishing | abdopublishing.com

WOMEN'S LIVES *in* *History*

abdopublishing.com

Published by Abdo Publishing, a division of ABDO, PO Box 398166, Minneapolis, Minnesota 55439. Copyright © 2017 by Abdo Consulting Group, Inc. International copyrights reserved in all countries. No part of this book may be reproduced in any form without written permission from the publisher. Essential Library™ is a trademark and logo of Abdo Publishing.

Printed in the United States of America, North Mankato, Minnesota
052016
092016

 THIS BOOK CONTAINS
RECYCLED MATERIALS

Cover Photo: Shutterstock Images
Interior Photos: Herman Verwey/Foto24/Gallo Images/Getty Images, 4–5; Herman Verwey/Foto24/Rex Features/AP Images, 7, 9; Rex Features/AP Images, 11; Christopher Halloran/Shutterstock Images, 15; Photobank Gallery/Shutterstock Images, 16–17; Image courtesy of DuPont, 19; NOAA, 20; Ned Alley/ZumaPress/Newscom, 23; Photos.com/Thinkstock, 25; Rick Mackler/ZumaPress/Newscom, 26–27; Jean-Marc Bouju/AP Images, 30–31; Vince Bucci/Getty Images, 32; David Bay/KRT/Newscom, 33; Alvaro Laiz - David Rengel/Transterra Media/Polaris/Newscom, 34–35; US Army RDECOM, 37; Susan Walsh/AP Images, 38–39; Owen/Black Star/Newscom, 43; Micheline Pelletier/Sygma/Corbis, 44–45; David Paul Morris/Bloomberg/Getty Images, 46; Rick Friedman/Corbis, 48–49; Nadine Rupp/Getty Images/Thinkstock, 52; MAXPPP/Newscom, 53; Smithsonian Institution Archives. Image # SIA2010-1511, 57; John D. & Catherine T. MacArthur Foundation, 58–59, 73, 81; NASA, 61, 67; US National Archives and Records Administration, 63; NASA/JPL-Caltech, 68–69; James S. Davis/US Navy, 75; Web Summit CC2.0, 76–77; Steve Jennings/TechCrunch/Getty Images, 83; Jagadeesh NV/EPA/Newscom, 85; Shutterstock Images, 87, 91; Evelyn Hockstein/Polaris/Newscom, 88–89; Aude Guerrucci-Pool/Getty Images, 92–93; Red Line Editorial, 96–97

Editor: Mirella Miller
Series Designer: Maggie Villaume

Cataloging-in-Publication Data
Names: Edwards, Sue Bradford, author.
Title: Women in science / by Sue Bradford Edwards.
Description: Minneapolis, MN : Abdo Publishing, [2017] | Series: Women's lives in history | Includes bibliographical references and index.
Identifiers: LCCN 2015960356 | ISBN 9781680782943 (lib. bdg.) | ISBN 9781680774887 (ebook)
Subjects: LCSH: Women scientists--Juvenile literature. | Women in science----Juvenile literature. | Women in the professions--Juvenile literature.
Classification: DDC 500--dc23
LC record available at http://lccn.loc.gov/2015960356

Contents

A scientist brings fossils out from Rising Star Cave.

CHAPTER ONE

The Women of Rising Star Cave

On October 7, 2013, an ad appeared on Facebook. It said:

> We need perhaps three or four individuals with excellent archaeological/
> paleontological and excavation skills for a short term project. . . . The catch
> is this—the person must be skinny and preferably small. They must not be
> claustrophobic, they must be fit, they should have some caving experience,
> climbing experience would be a bonus. They must be willing to work in
> cramped quarters.[1]

Lee Berger had posted the ad. No one knew what the job entailed, but everyone interested in early human fossils knew Berger. As a paleoanthropologist, he studies human ancestors dating back to 4.5 million years BCE. Berger explores the region known as the Cradle of Humankind in South Africa for fossils. He hopes these fossils will fill the gaps in information known about early people.

Marina Elliott felt as if the ad had been written for her. She was finishing her PhD at Simon Fraser University in British Columbia, Canada, and had already worked on excavations in Alaska and Siberia. "I was predisposed to extreme environments," she says. "Telling me that I'd have to do climbing, that it would be underground, and that it would be strange and potentially dangerous . . . it appealed."[2]

Berger expected very few applications, but 57 people from around the world responded within ten days.[3] Following a series of Skype interviews, Berger selected Elliott and five other female scientists. Elen Feuerriegel, K. Lindsay Eaves, Alia Gurtov, Hannah Morris, and Becca Peixotto would be joining Elliott. Women had once been discouraged from becoming scientists, but this group would soon help Berger make exciting discoveries.

Fossils Found

Because Berger had made a 2008 cave find in the Cradle of Humankind, he believed other local caves might house fossils as well. He asked South African cavers to keep their eyes open as they explored.

THE CRADLE OF HUMANKIND

Located in South Africa, the Cradle of Humankind is a United Nations World Heritage site. Scientists believe this is where humankind developed over a period of four million years. Forty percent of human ancestor fossils have been found in the Cradle of Humankind.[4] Other finds here include stone tools and fossils of plants and animals.

In Rising Star Cave in 2013, Steven Tucker and Rick Hunter climbed a rockfall that formed a steep ridge. Tucker slipped into a crack and pointed his toes to squeeze through the tight passage into a chamber. When Tucker saw bones on the floor, he realized

A small discovery by two cavers led Berger to a larger expedition in Rising Star Cave.

they were not from a bat or other small animal. He suspected they had found something important. Tucker photographed a jawbone before leaving the cave.

The cavers took this photo to Berger. Even from a photograph, Berger knew the bone belonged to a human relative. But Berger knew he could never slip through a passage that narrowed to seven inches (18 cm) wide.[5] He had to find scientists small enough, so he turned to social media to get the word out.

Before the crew could enter Rising Star Cave, cavers ran safety lines and fiber-optic cables, mounting cameras and lights. Only the six women would be allowed to enter the fossil chamber, but they would be accompanied as far as possible by cavers who would help ensure their safety. From above, Berger and other scientists would watch them work via the camera feeds, providing advice and help along the way.

Despite these precautions, the scientists would be making a hazardous climb. In recognition of their dedication to science, Berger nicknamed them the "underground astronauts."[6]

Fossils Brought to Light

Because the chamber was small, only three of the scientists would descend at a time. The first group to make the journey included Elliott, Peixotto, and Morris. When she first saw the chute that dropped into the bone-filled chamber, Elliott questioned taking the job. "It's a long crack, punctuated by shark-teeth protrusions. I remember looking down and thinking: I'm not sure I made the right decision."[7]

After making it through the chute, Elliott entered the chamber. It was topped with stalactites and smooth cave rock called flowstone. Below, on the ground, were the fossils. Elliott compared the sight with Egyptologist Howard Carter first gazing into the gold-filled treasure chamber of pharaoh Tutankhamen's unlooted tomb. When asked what he saw, Carter replied, "Things, wondrous things."[8] This time the scientists seeing wondrous things were women.

Fossils may look similar to stone, but they are fragile. To bring up the jawbone, the scientists slipped it into a plastic bag, wrapped the bag in Bubble Wrap, and placed the bundle in a plastic box. Elliott carried it to the surface, turning it over to Berger.

The original photo of the jawbone had no scale, so it was impossible to tell how big the fossil was. Because of this, Berger was surprised that it was much too small to be an *Australopithecus,* an extinct

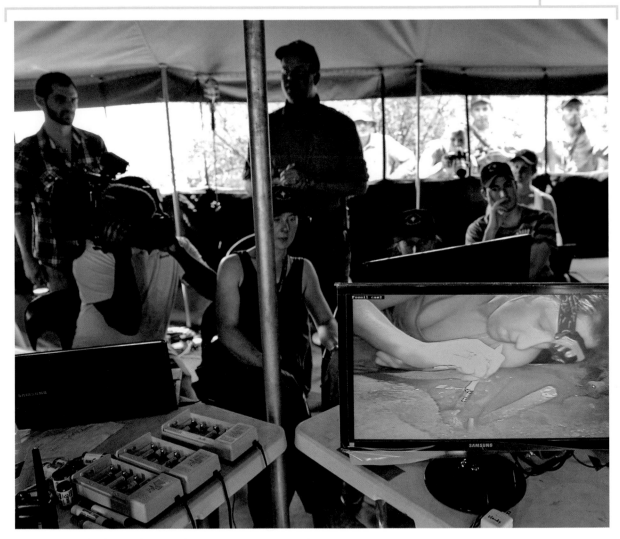

Scientists and paleontologists above ground guided the work of the scientists excavating Rising Star Cave below ground.

human ancestor that lived from two to four million years ago. It might have been from a previously unknown hominid group, but the scientists would need to bring up more bones in order to tell.

Descending again and again for three weeks, the scientists brought up bone after bone. They were bringing up pieces of several skeletons. The cave contained more fossils than anyone had seen in one place. Removing them was hard work. Normally, fossils are encased in stone under layers of dirt. In Rising Star Cave, approximately 400 fossils lay on the surface, and the scientists had to remove them without disturbing the fossils underneath. Only after removing the first 400 fossils did they reach fossils partially buried. The women swept the dirt away with small paintbrushes and removed all of the fossils in that layer before moving down to the next one. They worked slowly. But in 21 days, they recovered more than 1,500 bones from as many as 18 individuals.[9]

DARK ZONE SACRIFICE

Holley Moyes, a cave archaeologist at the University of California, Merced, studies ancient Mayan ruins throughout Belize, Guatemala, and Mexico. These caves contain sacrifices of pottery, tools, and even people. From 200 to 700 CE, the Maya left sacrifices near the mouths of the caves. From 700 to 900 CE, a time of drought, they sacrificed in the dark zone, areas unlit by the sun. Moyes thinks the Maya sacrificed in the dark zone because they believed that rain came from caves. Dark zone sacrifices might lure the rain out of the depths of the caves. Moyes continues to search Mayan caves for evidence to prove her theory.

What They Mean

As the scientists doing the excavation and other researchers examined the fossils, they realized they were looking at a combination of traits not previously seen. The bones belonged to a new human ancestor. Scientists determined

Scientists examine bone fragments found in Rising Star Cave.

the adults of this species stood less than five feet (1.5 m) tall.[10] They walked much as people do today, so their feet looked the same as modern feet. Their rounded skulls meant they were human, so the researchers named them *Homo naledi*. *Naledi* means "star" in Sesotho, a local South African language.

Because so many bones were found in one place, *Homo naledi* may be important. Rising Star Cave was not located at the bottom of a drop, similar to other fossil-rich caves, so the hominids did not fall in by accident. It was free of sediment, so the bones did not wash into the cave during a flood. Although predators create bone deposits, the *Homo naledi* remains show no tooth marks from a predator. Predators' deposits also contain bones from many animals, everything the predators ate over time. Except for a few mice and birds, this deposit was made up exclusively of *Homo naledi* bones. All of these factors mean Rising Star Cave may have been a burial spot.

Whether or not they had found the first human ancestors to bury their dead, Elliott, Feuerriegel, Eaves, Gurtov, Morris, and Peixotto filled in a blank on the human ancestral tree. But they are not the first women to make a name for themselves in paleoanthropology. Before them came Mary Leakey, a paleoanthropologist who made important finds in the Olduvai Gorge region of Tanzania. These women join Leakey and other scientists who laid the foundations for the study of humankind.

Women in Science

Throughout history, small numbers of women have been scientists. One of the earliest was Hypatia. She lived in Alexandria, now part of Egypt, in the 300s. An astronomer, she also wrote texts about mathematics.

THE GRANDAM OF PALEOANTHROPOLOGY

From 1935 to 1983, Mary Leakey hunted fossils in the Olduvai Gorge in Tanzania. She made many incredible finds during her research. In 1948, Leakey found a partial skull. *Proconsul africanus* lived more than 18 million years ago and was the first known primate from that time period, the Miocene Era. Leakey found another partial skull in 1959. Nearly two million years old, *Zinjanthropus boisei* was small-brained with huge teeth and heavy jaw muscles anchored to a skull ridge. Then, in 1979, Leakey discovered an 89-foot-(27 m) long trail of early human footprints. This 3.6-million-year-old trail was the first evidence of a bipedal ancestor who walked upright on two feet.[12]

Despite the discouragement of men, the tradition of women astronomers did not die. Throughout Europe in the 1600s and 1700s, women could not attend universities. But in Germany between 1650 and 1720, 14 percent of all astronomers were women.[11] To learn, they read whatever texts they could find.

Some women paid private tutors. They often worked with their brothers or husbands, leaving scholars unsure which women simply assisted the men and which studied the stars themselves.

Throughout this time, women researched and observed, reasoned and debated. Still, their accomplishments were often ignored. In part, this happened because many people believed women were incapable of science and their presence made men less capable as well.

In the early 1900s, women were finally allowed to study at graduate schools within the United States, and they earned PhDs in all scientific areas. Unfortunately, after World War II (1939–1945), women were once again forced out of most universities, a situation that was not reversed until the 1970s. Since then, women have been attending school and earning upper-level degrees in every scientific field.

Some of these scientists become academics, teaching at universities and doing research in the quest for new knowledge. Others research health, the environment, or energy and work for government agencies. Still others establish businesses in computing or medicine. Wherever they work, they use science to change the world and how people perceive it.

Why Women Should Be Scientists

President Barack Obama has firm opinions on why women need to work in science. "We've got half the population that is way underrepresented in those fields and that means that we've got a whole bunch of talent . . . not being encouraged the way they need to."[13] Science will continue to help the world grow and develop. The Obama administration knows that many different people and viewpoints are needed to move science forward. Supporting female scientists and increasing their opportunities will put the United States at the front of scientific discoveries.

These discoveries include research and testing. In the past, many scientific studies did not consider sex a variable during testing. Then scientists realized over time that male and female bodies react differently to medications or have different symptoms when experiencing an illness. Now the National Institutes of Health requires that sex is considered in testing.

Experts point out that women sometimes think differently than men. They believe that increasing the number of female scientists would change what topics are researched and what, in turn, is discovered. By adding the female perspective to scientific research, studies expand. It brings new and creative insights to projects. It also means more inventions can be studied and more breakthroughs can occur.

Having women in science goes beyond being the fair thing to do. It is also the smart thing to do.

World leaders, including President Obama, realize how important women are to the sciences.

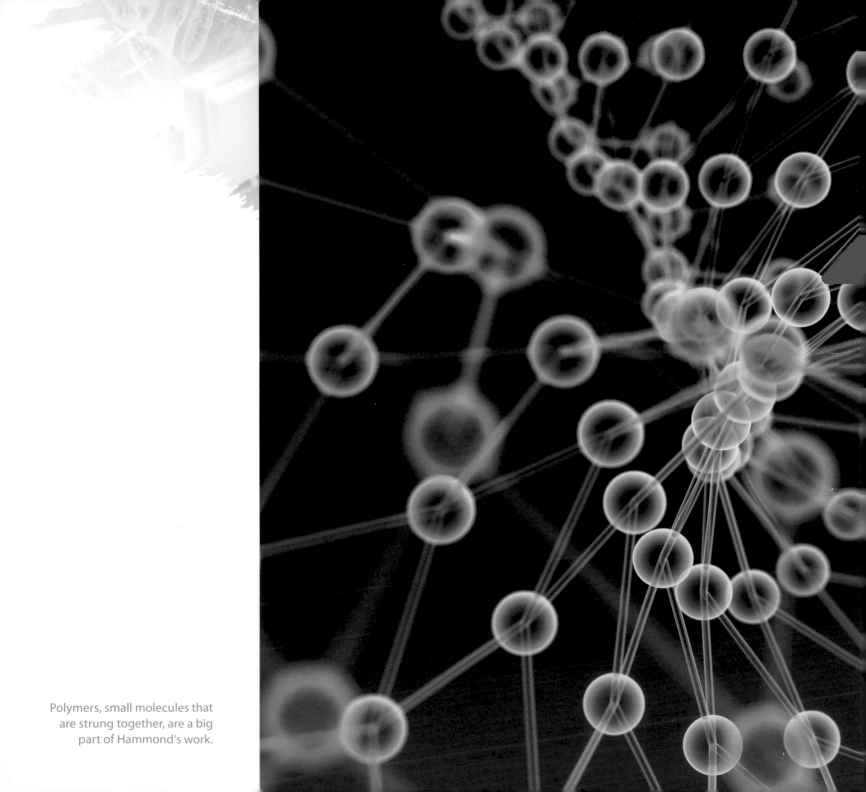

Polymers, small molecules that are strung together, are a big part of Hammond's work.

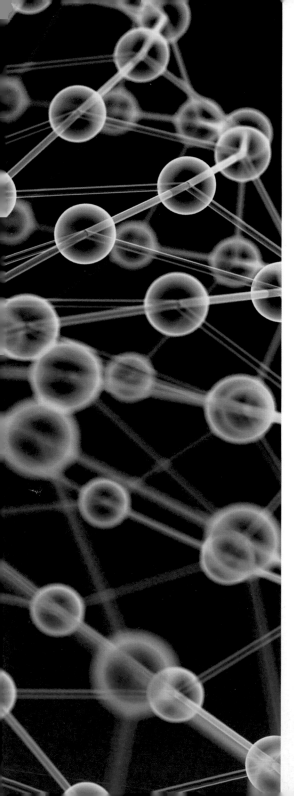

CHAPTER TWO

Women in Chemistry

P aula Hammond took chemistry in high school. When her teacher demonstrated how to combine two compounds to create something new, Hammond knew she wanted to be a chemist. Now she has her own lab at the David H. Koch Institute for Integrative Cancer Research at the Massachusetts Institute of Technology (MIT). She works with polymers, small molecules that are strung together.

In the 2000s, Hammond designed a polymer to give cancer patients their chemotherapy drugs. The polymer is a nanoparticle, so small it takes 1,000 particles to equal the width of a human hair. The polymer forms a bubble around the chemotherapy drug until the drug enters the tumor.

MIT provided a nurturing environment that helped Hammond be a successful chemist. She does the same for her students, encouraging them to find ways to solve problems with chemistry.

Hammond and other chemists study the properties of matter. Physical chemists study how matter and energy interact at the molecular level. Analytical chemists identify and measure physical and chemical properties. Biochemists study chemistry within living organisms. Organic chemists study materials that contain carbon, the element found in all living things. Inorganic chemists study metals and gases.

In the 1900s, chemistry was shaped by technologies that helped scientists view things at the molecular level. The space industry called on chemists to create materials that could stand up to extreme heat and cold. Although many teachers discouraged female students, some women still became chemists and are saving lives.

A Lifesaving Molecule

One of these women is physical chemist Stephanie Kwolek, who, similar to Hammond, worked with polymers. In 1965, Kwolek was working for DuPont to develop a fiber that would withstand extreme conditions. One day, she was working with polymers at very low temperatures when she noticed the molecules lined up to form a milky, crystalline solution.

Kwolek spun the strong, stiff solution into fibers, inventing Kevlar, a material five times stronger than steel but lighter than fiberglass. Its strength and light weight make Kevlar an ideal material for body armor, helmets, tires, sports equipment, and spacecraft.

In recognition of her efforts, Kwolek was inducted into the National Inventors Hall of Fame in 1994, only the fourth woman in history to be so honored.[1] In 1996, Kwolek accepted the National Medal of Technology and Innovation, followed by the Perkin Medal in 1997. Both are honors rarely awarded to women. Kwolek mentored

Kwolek developed the first liquid crystal polymer while working at DuPont.

other female scientists, offering them the encouragement and guidance they needed to pursue scientific careers.

Environmental Chemistry

Unlike physical chemists, analytical chemists often study the environment. In 1973, a University of California researcher discovered that chemicals called chlorofluorocarbons (CFCs), used in refrigerators and air conditioners, could destroy ozone, an oxygen compound. An ozone layer protects Earth and all life from the sun's ultraviolet rays. In 1983, scientists taking measurements in Antarctica found the continent's ozone levels had dropped by 35 percent.[2] CFCs were not used extensively in Antarctica. People refused to ban CFCs until they had more evidence.

Susan Solomon, a National Oceanic and Atmospheric Association chemist, provided that evidence. In 1986, she led an expedition to Antarctica and measured a chemical left behind when CFCs break down ozone. High levels of this chemical, even as ozone levels dropped, told Solomon and other scientists that CFCs were the culprit. With the evidence she provided, CFCs were banned by all countries belonging to the United Nations (UN).

Chemistry in Human Cells

Unlike Hammond, biochemist Jacqueline K. Barton did not take a single chemistry class in high school because it was not offered at the all-girls school she attended in the 1970s. Barton had her first class in college and chose chemistry as her major. As a graduate student, Barton studied deoxyribonucleic acid (DNA), the genetic material carried by all living things. She was one of the first people

AWFUL ARISTOTLE

Exclusive girls' schools such as the one Jacqueline K. Barton attended did not teach chemistry because at one time educators believed women could not be scientists. This idea can be traced back to the Greek philosopher Aristotle. In his book *Politics*, Aristotle wrote that women and men were permanently unequal. Men led and women followed. Women were passive and inferior. Being female should, according to Aristotle, be thought of as "a deformity."[3]

to realize DNA molecules conduct electricity.

The idea that DNA molecules conduct electricity was very controversial. Scientists argued about it in professional journals and at conferences. Barton did not let their questions stop her. Instead, she designed more experiments, ensuring the conditions under which she and her students tested DNA were identical to the conditions found in a human cell.

By 2004, Barton, now at the California Institute of Technology, had discovered that damaged DNA molecules no longer conduct electricity. The electric flow stops when one pair of proteins is substituted for another. Because cancer damages DNA, Barton hopes this finding will help doctors discover cancer-causing damage before the person develops cancer. Because of her work mentoring fellow chemists, Barton was given the American Institute of Chemists gold medal in 2015.

Brain Chemistry

Another leading biochemist is May-Britt Moser. Her parents did not attend a university, but her mother had dreamed of being a doctor. She encouraged her daughter to study and follow her passions. This led Moser to attend a university where professors encouraged her work. She and her husband,

Edvard, study the brain at their laboratory, the Kavli Institute for Systems Neuroscience and the Centre for the Biology of Memory at the Norwegian University of Science and Technology.

Because animals move from place to place, they need to know where they are in relation to other places. In 2005, Moser and her husband discovered that cells in a rat's brain act as an internal mapping system. They called these cells grid cells. These grid cells constantly create an updated map of where the rat has been and where it is at any given moment.

Grid cells have been found in primates, and scientists expect to find them in human beings. Scientists believe Moser's breakthrough may lead to discoveries about

Moser's groundbreaking discovery could help us better understand human memory.

how human memory works. This work is so groundbreaking that in 2014 Moser was awarded the Nobel Prize in Physiology or Medicine.

Cell Acidity

Yamuna Krishnan at the University of Chicago also works with cells. She finds ways to use nanomachines to show her what is happening within the cell itself. Similar to nanoparticles, nanomachines are microscopic. The nanomachines Krishnan works with are each made from three pieces of synthetic DNA that can pass into human cells. Whenever the short pieces of synthetic DNA are near each other, they self-assemble into a nanomachine.

The shape of the nanomachine changes with the acidity within the cell. Fluorescent tags of the nanomachine change from green to red. This helps scientists know acid is present. Cell acidity often accompanies a viral infection.

Nanomachines could also deliver medication. Today, medications are swallowed or injected, flooding the body. Medication wrapped in nanomachines could enter human cells and be released when the nanomachine changes shape, only medicating the infected cell. Before Krishnan's nanomachines can treat people, she must find a way for them to move safely through the body.

Chemists such as Hammond and Krishnan solve problems one step at a time. Whether they are treating illnesses, studying chemical processes in the body, or inventing new fibers, chemists use their understanding of how things interact to create solutions.

Marie Curie

The first female scientist many people name is Marie Curie. She left her home in Poland, journeying to Paris, France, in 1891, so she could study physics. In the late 1800s, women were not allowed to enroll in Polish universities.

While studying radioactivity in Paris, Curie and her husband, Pierre, extracted polonium and uranium from pitchblende, a black, tarry mineral made up almost entirely of uranium. The Curies realized these elements were what made this mineral radioactive. Because of their work, Curie and her husband earned a Nobel Prize in Physics in 1903. Curie was the first woman to receive this award.

After Pierre's death, Curie continued their work and took over his teaching position, becoming the first female teacher at the Sorbonne. Curie won a second Nobel Prize in 1911. This award was in chemistry for the couple's work in radiation, making her the first woman to win the Nobel Prize in both fields. Unfortunately, continual exposure to radiation took its toll, and Curie died in 1934. She has inspired many women and girls to study science and make discoveries of their own.

(1867–1934)

Williams, *middle*, studies
how to better understand
animals' habits.

CHAPTER THREE

Women in Biology

Terrie Williams is a biologist who studies ocean animals. She has attached video cameras to monk seals and whales so she can study animals in places humans cannot follow. Other biologists study the chemistry of life, plants, cells, ecology, evolution, genetics, animals, and animal behavior.

Williams, of the University of California, Santa Cruz, realized she needed to see the world as the animals see it when she was examining a dead sperm whale on a Hawaiian beach. Working with several local veterinarians, Williams set out to dissect the whale and find out what killed it. She checked the whale's 300-pound (136 kg) heart and its 18-pound (8.2 kg) brain but could find nothing wrong.[1] Reaching into the whale's stomach, Williams felt something hard. She pulled out a ball of plastic, followed by nine more similar balls. The balls were made up of netting and plastic line that had coiled into giant knots.

The whale could not see the free-floating net or line and had swallowed these things while hunting for squid. The tangled plastic had filled its stomach and eventually starved the animal to death. Williams realized scientists could not understand the problems animals face if they could not follow the animals. She began using cameras to see what the animals saw.

In 2000, Williams mounted video cameras on the backs of aquatic mammals, including a bottlenose dolphin, an elephant seal, and a blue whale. She studied how animals conserve energy and oxygen when diving to great depths for long periods of time. Williams discovered that animals follow a powerful dive with a less intense glide.

The 1900s saw many advances in the study of biology with a greater emphasis on experiments and direct observation. An understanding of DNA and how it works changed how biologists think about all living things. This was also when people began to understand the impact of pollution and scientists first studied how to reverse these effects. Women have

WET WORKS

Paris dressmaker Jeanne Villepreux-Power gave up sewing for science when she married a merchant and they moved to Italy. Observing cephalopods, a group of mollusks that includes the octopus, squid, and nautilus, Villepreux-Power discovered that octopuses use tools. She also discovered how the paper nautilus builds its own shell. To watch these animals closely, in 1832 she invented a trio of boxes called aquariums. One glass box was made to hold creatures indoors. A glass box inside a cage sat in shallow water for outdoor observation. The last was a cage anchored to the seafloor. Thanks to Villepreux-Power, people can keep fish in their homes or visit aquariums large enough to permanently house octopuses.

worked in biology for many years, warning people about pollution, observing wildlife, and more.

Chimp Champion

Jane Goodall did not plan to become a scientist. She did not have the money for college. Her mother told her to become a secretary, because secretaries are needed all around the world. In addition to being able to support herself, her inquisitive daughter would get to travel. Goodall worked a variety of jobs, saving her money so she could visit a friend in Kenya.

In Kenya, she met Louis Leakey, a scientist who wanted someone to help study chimpanzees. Leakey thought Goodall would be perfect for the job because she was not a trained scientist. Without a science background, she would find her own way of doing things and learn something new.

Goodall traveled to Tanganyika, now Tanzania, to live among and observe the chimpanzees. The scientific community, made up largely of men, was shocked. This was not how things were done, and an untrained woman might put herself in danger.

SILENT SPRING

Rachel Carson grew up within 20 miles (32 km) of Pittsburgh, Pennsylvania, a major industrial center where factories polluted the air and water. This made her alert to environmental damage. As a biologist, she saw the harm the insecticide DDT was doing around the United States. *Reader's Digest* refused to publish her pieces on dying wildlife and polluted water. The publishers thought their readers, primarily housewives, were too emotionally delicate for this topic. But eventually, excerpts from her upcoming book, *Silent Spring*, were published in the *New Yorker* in 1962. The book blamed government researchers and politicians for policies that led to widespread use of DDT. Congress banned DDT, and Carson's writing gave birth to the environmental activist movement.

When Goodall began her study in 1960, scientists believed that only people used tools. Goodall saw a chimpanzee use a blade of grass to fish insects out of a termite mound. She saw another chimpanzee strip the leaves off a twig so it could use the twig to fish for termites. Chimpanzees made and used tools. Goodall changed how scientists studied animals and how they saw chimpanzees and humankind.

Among the Elephants

In 1972, Cynthia Moss learned from Goodall's techniques and applied them to studying African elephants. Today, Moss and her team continue to study 50 elephant families in 400 square miles (1,000 sq km) of the Amboseli National Park in Kenya.[2]

Each elephant family is made up of a matriarch, or elder female leader, and her daughters and their children. Moss and her crew learned the importance of matriarchs to survival. The older the elephant, the more experience she has in telling friend from foe and recalling where to feed.

In addition to studying the elephants themselves, Moss works to keep them from being hunted to extinction. Elephant tusks are one of the main sources

PRIMATES FIRST

Because primates include humans, biologists called primatologists hope to learn about the animals, but also about early humans. In addition to Goodall's work among the chimpanzees, Dian Fossey studied the endangered mountain gorillas of Rwanda until her murder in 1985. Birute Mary Galdikas has studied Indonesia's orangutans since 1971.

Moss's work in the field is dedicated to stopping poachers.

of ivory. Moss first fought to ban ivory sales in 1989. Now she works to stop poachers who come into Amboseli and kill the elephants to take their tusks. The poachers sell the tusks on the illegal ivory market. Moss has devoted her life to saving the elephants. "I don't do anything else," Moss said. "If I had to do this over I would."[3]

Cracking Cholera

While biologists such as Moss work in the field, other biologists work with data in the lab. Mercedes Pascual works with complex systems models at the University of Chicago. A complex system is made up of a large number of things that affect each other because they are interconnected. An ecosystem, such as the ocean, is a complex system. Pascual creates mathematical models of the systems she wants to study so she can see which events repeatedly occur, one following the other.

Pascual's work in systems models led to the 2000 discovery that El Niño, a winter warming of the Pacific Ocean, leads to cholera outbreaks in Bangladesh. Cholera is caused by a bacterium that lives with other microscopic animals in salty waters where a river and the sea come together. When people drink water with microscopic animals living in it, they may be at risk of catching cholera. El Niño increases the water temperature, which allows these small animals to thrive.

Pascual and her colleagues discovered this correlation when they compared records on cholera outbreaks and climate. They found that climate change and changes in El Niño correspond closely with an increase

In 2002, *Discover* magazine named Pascual one of the 50 most important women in science.

An African giant pouched rat searches for land mines in Tanzania.

in cholera cases. This is the first quantitative evidence that proves climate change is also changing the rates of infectious diseases.

Scientists know it is not weather alone that determines the number of cholera outbreaks. Other factors include clean water, general health, and the size of the population. But knowing that weather is a component can put health officials on high alert when conditions are right for cholera to thrive.

Rat Detectors

In addition to studying animals in the wild, biologists study animals that work with people. In 2012, Cornell animal behaviorist Danielle Lee started studying bomb-sniffing rats. Training one African giant pouched rat takes between eight and twelve months.[4] Trainers continue despite the risk of failure, because it is estimated these rats have cleared Mozambique of 6,693 land mines, 29,934 small arms and ammunition, and 1,087 bombs left after the country's civil war.[5]

Lee wants to make the program even better. Rats are already the best animals for the job because they are low to the ground and have a strong sense of smell. They do not get attached to specific trainers, which means the animals can be sent wherever they are needed. By understanding the animals themselves, Lee hopes to breed them to be even better sniffers. She also hopes to come up with new and improved ways to train them.

Micromanagement

As with Pascual, Christina Agapakis works with organisms too small to see. This biologist is a pioneer in the new field of synthetic biology, which combines molecular biology, chemistry, and engineering. This is how Agapakis explains her work:

> What can organisms do as part of a community that they can't do alone? I'm fascinated by how the biochemistry of individual bacteria changes when they are part of a community, especially because so much of what we know about microbes comes from bacteria studied in isolation and we still know so little about how microbes work together with other bacteria and with our bodies.[6]

Agapakis sees this field revolutionizing fuels, foods, and medicines. For example, not all digestive problems respond to medications, but what if scientists could change the microbes living in a patient's gut? Usually, doctors think only about treating the patient. Agapakis's way of looking at things includes not only the patient but also the microbes that normally live inside the patient. Whether they work in the lab, crunch numbers on a computer, or study animals in the wild, these scientists are looking at creative ways to solve problems and changing how people look at the world.

Kiki Sanford

Kirsten "Kiki" Sanford has a PhD in physiology from the University of California, Davis. Although she does research and publishes on her specialty, memory and learning in birds, she realized she wanted to teach the public about science.

In 1999, Sanford started a radio show, *This Week in Science*, which is broadcast each week from the university. Now also a podcast, the show explains the latest and greatest research and discoveries in a way everyday people can understand.

This Week in Science isn't Sanford's only project. She also hosts the podcast *Potential Energy*, which focuses on alternative energy. She can also be seen online in *Dr. Kiki's Science Hour*. Whether viewers catch her videos or her podcasts, they come away from the program with a better understanding of the world in which they live.

(1974–)

Doudna speaks at the 2015
International Summit on
Human Gene Editing.

CHAPTER FOUR

Women in Genetics and Medicine

In 2012, Jennifer Doudna, a geneticist who studies genes and heredity at the University of California, Berkeley, published an article about the CRISPR process. Through this process, bacteria copy and save virus genes. This means the bacterium will recognize and defend itself if the same virus ever infects it again.

Using the CRISPR process, scientists can cut and save individual genes. This allows the scientists to model human diseases in mice, isolate single genes for study, and alter multiple genes at one time to study how the genes work together. It makes it easier to develop gene therapies to aid in the treatment of various diseases, including cystic fibrosis and AIDS.

The ease with which genes can be substituted worries many scientists. Not all cuts are made precisely and accurately. Changing one gene can alter an organism in unexpected ways. There is a debate about whether this process should be allowed at all. Doudna agrees there are dangers, but she also sees benefits. She believes the United States needs to take the lead in providing information about the benefits and risks of this technique. Doudna also wants the United States to draft new safety guidelines for scientists.

Genetic scientists study how traits are passed from parent to child. Geneticists study individual genes, DNA, and even how to use genes to treat diseases.

Compared with many sciences, genetics is a young field, developed almost entirely in the last 100 years. Scientists did not understand the structure of DNA until it was revealed in a series of photographs Rosalind Franklin took in 1953. As scientists learned to cut genes from one organism and insert them into the DNA of another,

PICTURING DNA

After studying at the University of Cambridge in London, England, Rosalind Franklin spent three years in Paris at the Laboratoire Central des Services Chimiques de l'État. There she learned X-ray diffraction techniques, which gather information on the structure of a crystal or other microscopic form. In 1951, Franklin returned to England and took the first X-ray photographs of DNA. These photos revealed DNA's double-helix structure. Before she could publish her findings, a colleague, Maurice Wilkins, showed another scientist, James Watson, her photographs. Watson rushed to publish his new understanding of DNA's structure, beating Franklin to it. Wilkins had always treated Franklin as an inferior. To this day, some people question whether Franklin truly made the 1953 discovery or if she simply assisted the male researchers.

they questioned what limits should be put on the work, leading to the first guidelines, in 1972. Genetics often overlaps with other medical researchers. Female scientists today carry on the work begun by Franklin and other pioneers.

Women's Cancers

Doudna is not the only geneticist who has stirred up controversy with her work. In 1973, at the University of California, Berkeley, Mary-Claire King showed that a human gene and the corresponding chimpanzee gene are, on average, 99 percent identical.[1] Obviously, the differences between the two organisms are visible, but on the genetic level the differences are quite small.

King continued studying human genes, sequencing the genes of remote populations worldwide. In 1990, she discovered BRCA1. Mutations to this gene can cause both breast and ovarian cancer in generation after generation of related women. Understanding what may cause breast cancer in certain populations of women helps these women make educated decisions about their health and possible treatments.

HITTING A NERVE

Ida Hyde's family paid to educate their sons, but not their daughters. At 24 years old, Hyde attended college for one year and then became a teacher. She eventually graduated from Cornell University in 1891 with a degree in physiology, the study of the body and how it works. Hyde studied animals' nervous, circulatory, and respiratory systems. In 1920, she invented the microelectrode, which could add chemicals to a cell and simultaneously measure the cell's electric current. A less fragile version of this tool proved vital to the study of nerve cells.

Tilghman, *front*, was part of the team that successfully cloned the first gene from a mammal.

Tilghman realized that male and female genes could be unequally expressed. This means that sometimes a gene for a trait can be seen in the parent but is unseen or silent in the offspring. Scientists refer to this ability to be unexpressed as imprinting.

Imprinted genes often involve growth. Tilghman found if a mouse inherits the equivalent of two paternal copies of a certain gene, it is 130 percent as large as its littermates. Mice with two maternal genes are 60 percent of the size of the average mouse.[3]

Scientists study imprinting because it has been associated with several human diseases, including manic-depressive illness, Angelman syndrome, which affects the nervous system, and Prader-Willi syndrome, which affects appetite and intelligence. Scientists such as Tilghman are studying unequal expression in hopes of finding the cures needed to help people live healthy lives.

Boney Benefits

Other scientists are finding ways to use a patient's genes to restore that person's health. Nina Tandon has developed a way to grow human bone from a patient's own stem cells. Stem cells have not specialized into bone cells, muscle cells, or nerve cells. Stem cells divide and replace cells within a person's bone marrow throughout his or her life.

Each year, approximately 900,000 Americans require bone-related surgery.[4] Some have been in accidents, others are cancer patients, and still others are correcting a problem with which they were born. These patients have two choices. Surgery can be done using bone

Tandon grew up taking objects apart and rebuilding them, leading her to pursue an engineering degree.

from a person who died, which may be diseased. Or their own bone can be used, but this increases their pain and chance of infection and nerve damage.

To grow bone, Tandon's company, EpiBone, harvests stem cells from the patient's fat tissue. Under the right laboratory conditions, stem cells become specialized cells such as bone cells. At EpiBone, the stem cells are used to grow a bone in the shape and size needed. It takes approximately three weeks to grow a new bone. The process is expensive and still awaiting government approval, but the promise it holds to improve lives is vast. Says Tandon, "Isn't it exciting to think that if the first industrial revolution was about machines, the second was about information, that the third revolution could be about life itself."[5] Genetic scientists, such as Doudna and Tandon, work in the lab to understand how these building blocks of life affect health and healing.

SAFETY FIRST

Biologist Maxine Singer watched fellow scientists develop lab-created or recombinant DNA. She worried about the health dangers posed if engineered organisms escaped from the lab into the environment. In 1975, Singer led a National Institutes of Health conference of 150 scientists who drafted safety guidelines for genetic engineering.[6] These guidelines demanded protective measures ranging from gloves to extractor hoods, a type of vented fan. Some experiments were banned altogether.

Hau uses her physics
background to work on slowing
and stopping light.

CHAPTER FIVE

Women in Physics

I n 1999, Lene Hau led a team of physicists in slowing and stopping a beam of light. It is something Albert Einstein said was possible in theory, although most scientists did not believe anyone would ever succeed in doing it.

Most types of matter interact with light in one of three ways. Materials such as glass allow the light to pass through. Mirrorlike materials reflect the light. And items such as a book, which are neither reflective nor transparent, absorb the light.

To stop light, Hau had to create something that would slow it down to the point that it stopped moving. To create this substance, Hau cooled sodium atoms until they were only a few degrees warmer than absolute zero, the coldest temperature possible, −460 degrees Fahrenheit (−273°C). This is colder than anything in nature, even in deep space. Atoms almost stop moving. When Hau shone lasers onto these super cold atoms, the light slowed and then stopped completely. Scientists believe this discovery will eventually revolutionize computers and communications.

Hau's parents believed that, like her brother, she should follow her passions, which led her to study math and physics although men dominate the field. Physics is the study of matter and energy and how they affect each other. Physicists study things smaller than atoms and as vast as the universe. Cosmologists study the origins of the universe and how it has changed. Astrophysicists study galaxies, planets, and everything that moves through space. Geophysicists study the earth and how it works. Atomic physicists study the atom, whereas nuclear physicists focus on the atom's nucleus.

The biggest changes in physics have come in the last century with the understanding of quantum mechanics, or how atoms and the particles that make them up interact and move. In the latter part of the 1900s, more women, such as Hau, have entered the field.

SPLITTING THE ATOM

In 1938, Otto Hahn and Fritz Strassmann were performing an experiment with radioactive uranium when a different element, barium, appeared. Hahn wrote to Lise Meitner and challenged her to explain how this could happen. Meitner realized that Hahn and Strassmann had split the uranium atoms' nuclei, releasing energy and forming barium. She published her theory, but the male scientists received the Nobel Prize in Chemistry.

Additional Dimensions

One scientist trying to understand the origin of the universe is Lisa Randall, a Harvard University physicist working in string theory. String theory states that everything is composed of tiny vibrating strings of energy. The strings do not vibrate in only the four dimensions of length, width, height, and time. For this theory to work, the strings have to vibrate in a vast number of additional dimensions, called branes or membranes.

Randall has worked with branes since 1998. When someone does not understand these extra dimensions, Randall has one explanation. Things that are stuck on the two-dimensional surface of a shower curtain are in three-dimensional space, even if the shower curtain and the scum only use two of these dimensions. The three-dimensional universe would be the shower curtain within a universe with additional dimensions.

New Forms of Matter

While Randall looks at the universe as a whole, other physicists study particles that make up atoms. There are two basic types of particles, bosons and fermions. Electrons, protons, and neutrons are fermions. Photons are bosons. They differ in how they move, which affects how they behave.

Randall is part of a Harvard task force
focusing on why so few women
enter science.

On June 5, 1995, physicists Carl Wieman and Eric Cornell chilled bosons to the point that they created a new form of matter called the Bose-Einstein condensate. They won a Nobel Prize in Physics, and the race was on to create a new form of matter with fermions.

The problem to be overcome was what happens when fermions are cooled. Unlike bosons, which cluster together, fermions repel each other. Deborah Jin and her team at the National Institute of Standards and Technology, part of the US Department of Commerce, overcame fermions' tendency to push each other away by using lasers and magnetic fields. Jin and her team used these tools to force the fermions to pair up. Once paired, the fermions behaved similarly to bosons and combined. On December 16,

Jin's team made amazing discoveries in the world of matter.

lasting one-billionth of one-billionth of a second. Unlike many massive laser facilities, Murnane's rig fits on a dining room table.

Other scientists produce lasers by accelerating electrons, but Murnane combines many visible light frequencies. This produces a high-speed, short-burst laser that, as an X-ray, permits scientists to view electrons moving around atoms.

Murnane encourages students to think of themselves as people seeking to make discoveries, explaining to them that they are students until they find something new. Once they make a discovery and understand its importance, they have become scientists. Whether they study something as vast as the universe or as minute as a boson, physicists are expanding people's understanding of everything in the universe.

Chien-Shiung Wu

During World War II, Chien-Shiung Wu worked on the Manhattan Project, helping produce the US military's first nuclear weapons. As part of this project, she developed a process for enriching uranium, making it usable as fuel for nuclear reactions.

Chien-Shiung continued her work in physics at Columbia University after the war. In 1956, her male colleagues Tsung-Dao Lee and Chen Ning Yang proposed a theory that contradicted physics' parity law. This law states that objects that are mirror images of each other behave identically.

Chien-Shiung came up with the experiment that disproved the parity law, spinning radioactive cobalt-60 nuclei at low temperatures. If the parity law was correct, electrons would shoot off in paired directions, but that is not what happened. Although the American Association of University Women lauded her experiment in the press, the Nobel committee gave the prize to her male colleagues. Chien-Shiung became the first woman president of the American Physical Society in 1975. She acknowledged the discrimination she faced, but encouraged other women to pursue careers in science.

(1912–1997)

Seager is a leader among
scientists who study the stars,
planets, and space beyond
Earth's atmosphere.

CHAPTER SIX

Women and Space

S hortly before her fortieth birthday, in 2011, Sara Seager, a planetary scientist at MIT, called together a group of colleagues. "Hundreds or thousands of years from now, when people look back at our generation, they will remember us for being the first people who found the Earth-like worlds," Seager said. "I've convened all of you here because we want to make an impact and we want to make that happen. We are on the verge of being those people, not individually but collectively."[1]

Working at her request, in 2014, scientists using the Kepler space telescope discovered 715 new planets around distant stars. This brought the number of discovered planets orbiting stars other than our sun to 1,693.[2]

It is not enough to find other planets. Seager is driven to find an earthlike planet capable of supporting life. Unfortunately, many of these new planets are too far away to easily study. Seager is working on the Transiting Exoplanet

Survey Satellite (TESS), which, beginning in 2017, will search for planets that are close enough to observe for signs of life.

Seager's father, a doctor, wanted her to study medicine so she could support herself. He scolded her when she chose a different path. But she does not let other people's attitudes slow her down. "It's so liberating not to care about what other people are thinking."[3]

Astronomers observe these planets through telescopes. They use physics and create computer programs to analyze the data they gather. Space travel has allowed scientists to put telescopes in space. This and computers, which can handle large amounts of data, have changed astronomy in the last century. Scientists can see more than ever before and have help crunching the data. Unfortunately, as in physics, female scientists have had to struggle to play a part either as astronauts or as astronomers.

Star Bright

Astronomer Nancy Grace Roman is the mother of the Hubble Space Telescope, a project that took her from the early 1960s until 1990 to complete. After Roman earned her PhD in astronomy in 1949, she worked for the US Naval Research Observatory. Although she enjoyed researching stars and teaching, it was almost impossible at that time for a woman to be a high-ranking professor. She focused on research and was soon the head of the microwave spectroscopy section, using microwaves to study stars. The National Aeronautics and Space Administration (NASA) liked Roman's work and asked if she

Roman helped create satellites during her time at NASA.

knew someone who could head a new space astronomy program. Eventually, they gave the job to Roman herself.

Astronomers observing space from Earth must contend with the planet's atmosphere, which is full of dust, heat waves, and clouds. Looking at the stars and planets through the atmosphere is similar to looking through cloudy, rippled glass. That is why astronomers decided the best thing to do would be to place a telescope above the atmosphere, either on a satellite or on the moon.

NASA wanted the telescope to have a human crew, but astronomers wanted it to be computerized. A human manually operating the scope would require an atmosphere. This same human might move, and movement when the telescope was taking photographs would be transmitted as vibrations and blur the photographs. The need for an atmosphere was part of what the astronomers were trying to escape.

As a scientist, Roman understood the problems and could mediate between what astronomers wanted and what NASA engineers saw as possible. The final plan reduced the size of the telescope's mirror and thus the telescope itself, and opted for an unmanned system on a satellite versus a telescope with a crew. The Hubble Space Telescope satellite went into space on board the space shuttle *Discovery* on April 24, 1990. In addition to the Hubble Space Telescope, Roman designed satellite instruments that gathered information about the sun, helping further the understanding of our star.

Scientists in Space

Roman wasn't the only scientist to be drawn in by NASA. Sally Ride had a doctorate in astrophysics, but she never considered becoming an astronaut until she saw a NASA advertisement. NASA had not trained any new astronauts since the late 1960s Apollo program that landed US astronauts on the moon. Only 30 of these astronauts remained active when Ride saw the ad.[4] The Apollo astronauts were all men and were former military pilots, because all astronauts needed to be able to pilot the Apollo command modules.

Ride made history by becoming an astronaut in the 1970s.

TZOs form when a red supergiant, an aging giant star, engulfs a nearby neutron star, the smallest star type. A TZO appears to be an ordinary red supergiant until an astronomer examines its spectrum. The churning atmosphere in a TZO includes chemicals found not in red supergiants, but in neutron stars. These show in the spectrum, but only if someone looks for them. For 40 years, TZOs existed only in theory.

In 2014, while examining stars within the Milky Way and the Magellanic Clouds, galaxies visible from Earth's Southern Hemisphere, Levesque spotted a red supergiant that had a much greater mass than such a star should have. Then she looked at its spectrum and saw lithium, molybdenum, and rubidium—a combination not normally found in a red supergiant.

Levesque is not claiming to have found a TZO. Instead, she calls her discovery a candidate. "We're calling [it] a 'candidate' for a reason," Levesque cautions. "Claiming that we've found a totally new model of star is an extraordinary claim, it requires extraordinary proof."[7] Despite this humble attitude, *Business Insider* has named Levesque one of the 15 most amazing women in science today.[8]

The Woman in Charge

Before becoming an astronaut, Ellen Ochoa studied optical systems for information processing. She is coinventor of an optical inspection system, a method for optical object recognition, and a way to remove random blotches from images.

In 1993, Ochoa became the first Hispanic-American female astronaut in space. She flew aboard the space shuttle *Discovery* when the crew was studying Earth's ozone layer. A veteran of four flights, she logged more than 950 hours in space and worked to develop software, computer hardware, and robotics.[9]

Since 2012, Ochoa has been director of the Johnson Space Center in Houston, Texas. It is the mission control center for all US manned space flights and also a major research and development facility.

In her current position, Ochoa influences the work of both astronomers and astronauts.

Howell's work was imperative in the launch of the *Genesis* satellite.

CHAPTER SEVEN

Women in Mathematics and Engineering

K athleen Howell at Purdue University has pioneered a way to use gravitational fields to move spacecraft using little or no fuel. Each planet or other large body in space exerts gravity, pulling nearby objects toward it. The area around a planet in which this happens is its gravitational field. Howell's technique involves exploiting libration points. Earth and the sun share five libration points. This means there are five points in space where the pull from Earth's gravitational force is equal to the pull from the sun's gravitational force.

There is no marker showing where these libration points are. They are mathematical concepts. Calculating the location of these points requires balancing the gravity and the centrifugal force of the objects, such as Earth and the sun.

Because of this balance between forces, movement from one libration point to another requires very little fuel. Scientists refer to the pathway between these points as the Interplanetary Superhighway. It is how asteroids, comets, and even dust move freely throughout the galaxy. Howell realized this pathway offered the opportunity to move spacecraft without using as much fuel. Although using this method would reduce fuel costs, traveling without using engines means traveling at a slow rate of speed that could easily be topped by a traditional rocket engine.

Howell first used this method for the 2001 *Genesis* launch to study the sun. The libration point Howell used for this mission is nearly one million miles (1.6 million km) from Earth, toward the sun.[1] *Genesis* orbited this point and collected solar wind samples.

Howell tells girls that studying math will open up many possibilities for them. That said, she ultimately recommends they follow their dreams.

MORE THAN A PRETTY FACE

Classic movie fans know Hedy Lamarr as a beautiful actress, but in the early days of World War II she was coinventor of the Secret Communication System, patented in 1942. It used regularly changing radio frequencies to guide a remote-controlled torpedo. The frequency changes made it much harder to jam. The technology is the basis of today's Bluetooth and Wi-Fi connections.

Mathematics is the science of numbers and their operations. It is also the study of patterns. Mathematicians study how numbers relate to each other and how they combine. Some mathematicians specialize in geometry, the study of space. They study measurements and abstract shapes and concepts. Mathematicians in the 1900s explored sets, or groups of related numbers, theories in algebra and pure mathematics, the science of numbers, quantities, and space as theory. Some mathematicians today work simply to acquire new knowledge. Others work to solve concrete problems.

Anyone who uses the Internet or takes and sends photos with a smartphone benefits from Ingrid Daubechies's work. She made a discovery while studying mathematical models called wavelets. Wavelets are oscillations, or regular variations, that form a repeating pattern that moves up and down similar to a wave. Wavelets can be tall or short, varying in strength or amplitude, and wide or narrow, varying in frequency and duration.

In 1987, while studying signals at Bell Labs, Daubechies discovered a new variety of wavelet, which is now named after her. Daubechies wavelets are described mathematically as orthogonal. They are tiny digital fragments that allow digital information, such as a photograph, to be broken up into smaller, more manageable bits, for both transmission and analysis.

Daubechies explains to people that her wavelets are similar to brushstrokes. The more brushstrokes that are in a painting, the clearer and more complex is the image. And the more wavelets that are in a set of data, the clearer and more crisp is the final photograph.

In addition to breaking the image into manageable bits, oscillations can be compressed, making it easier and faster to send large amounts of information such as a digital photo. The reassembled image is crisper and cleaner than a digital image created and sent without using these wavelets. This process is called a wavelet transform, and it works through quantizing, which is similar to rounding numbers.

Daubechies became the first woman to win the National Academy of Sciences Award in Mathematics in 2000. She won it for her work in making wavelets a basic tool of mathematics that is used in science.

MODERN MOTION

Lillian Moller Gilbreth and her husband studied scientific management principles. He was interested in efficiency on the factory floor and consulted with companies on how to improve productivity. Gilbreth was more interested in the people and worked to improve worker safety, health, and motivation. In 1924, she did motion studies on thousands of women in their homes so she could improve how kitchens were laid out and designed. She held patents on an electric mixer, refrigerator shelving, and foot pedals that opened trash can lids. Gilbreth was the first woman to belong to the American Society of Mechanical Engineers and was called "a genius in the art of living."[2]

Perfect Graphs

Not all mathematicians work on things with obvious applications. Some prefer the puzzles of pure mathematics. Maria Chudnovsky studies graph theory, but not just graphs with x- and y-axes. Her graphs

Chudnovsky graphs complicated theories.

contain a bunch of dots with some dots connected by lines. The way Chudnovsky explains it is to imagine each computer on the Internet as a dot. If two computers can "talk" directly to each other, a line connects them.[3]

At Princeton in 2002, she helped prove the perfect-graph theory, which says "only two kinds of flaws can make a graph imperfect."[4] This mathematical puzzle had been around since the 1960s, but no one had been able to prove it. Chudnovsky and her team showed that each perfect graph fit into one of five groups, and that either flaw would place a graph outside these groups.

Chudnovsky does not worry about real-world applications for her work. She wants to figure out the answers to the puzzles put before her. And what is her advice to young scientists who think they might be interested in mathematics? "It teaches us to think abstractly," she says. "If you think math is what you want to do, give it a chance."[5]

Predicting Crime

Some mathematicians use data about the past to predict the future. In 2010, Andrea Bertozzi of the University of California, Los Angeles, and her team developed computer models to predict criminal activity.

They based their models on statistics for crime for a ten-year period. The models began with measureable empirical data. For burglaries, the data consisted of which homes were broken into and when. Did one break-in lead to three more nearby? If so, it would appear in the data.

Running the computer model produces a changing map as areas of activity bloom and then die out, but the model isn't entirely accurate. When Bertozzi runs the model for crime and then the police model, the crime may shift to a nearby area. In reality, criminal activity died out completely when the police made arrests. With more information, Bertozzi hopes to create a model that police departments and other groups can use in planning.

Grace Murray Hopper

Anyone who worked with US Navy programmer Grace Murray Hopper knew better than to say, "That's the way we've always done it."[6] Hopper often reminded her coworkers of the need to innovate and believed so strongly in this point that her office clock ran counterclockwise.

Hopper was 34 years old and teaching math at Vassar College when the Japanese bombed Pearl Harbor, Hawaii, in 1941. She wanted to help her country, so she joined the Naval Reserves.

The navy immediately put Hopper to work on the Harvard Mark I computer. This early computer, which was 51 feet (15.5 m) long and weighed five short tons (4.5 metric tons), was known as a mechanical calculator, or the Automatic Sequence Controlled Calculator.[7] Hopper created a 561-page manual outlining the most important ways these computing machines could be used. She created instructional sequences, which were actually early examples of digital computer programming.

Hopper worked as the director of the Navy Programming Language Standards Group, developing its data processing abilities. In 1985, she was promoted to rear admiral, the first woman to achieve this rank. In 1986, she retired but continued to teach and give talks, using visual aids to help people understand computer sciences.

(1906–1992)

Breazeal was listed as one of *Entrepreneur* magazine's women to watch in 2015.

CHAPTER EIGHT

Women in Computing and Robotics

I n the 1990s, Cynthia Breazeal was working toward her PhD when she joined the Mobile Robots group, or Mobot Lab, at MIT. There she helped develop two insect-like robots called Hannibal and Attila. These light, durable machines could be sent as a group to explore Mars. Although NASA ultimately did not choose these machines, these robots influenced NASA as it developed the *Sojourner* rover, which rolled onto Mars on July 6, 1997. As *Sojourner* explored Mars, Breazeal realized that although robotics had made it to a distant planet, robots still had not made it into people's homes.

This thought caused Breazeal to switch her PhD focus. Before people would want home robots, they would need to be comfortable with them. So

customers out of thousands of dollars. Mather did not want to simply react to the criminals. She wanted to get ahead of them.

Mather could not do that at eBay, because businesses in the early 2000s did not focus on preventing computer crime. They thought it was better to react after the fact. Despite this, Mather moved forward and founded her security company, Silver Tail Systems, in 2008.

In less than ten years, companies have realized how important online security is, and they are willing to pay Mather to solve their problems. Her job is not easy. Every time she makes a security change, she needs to think ahead to what the criminals will do next. If she does not, the criminals may come up with a plan that is even more damaging than what they were doing before.

Others have recognized Mather's work as well. In 2012, she was sixth on *Fortune*'s list of the most powerful women entrepreneurs and ninth on *Business Insider*'s list of the 25 most powerful women engineers.[3]

ROBOT VISION

In 1988, Ruzena Bajcsy realized robotic perception needed to be active. Until her discovery, robots imaged the world through fixed cameras, sampled data, and came to conclusions. Instead of simply seeing, they needed to look, focus when necessary, and even change angle and distance, not just recording but also interacting with their environment.

Robotic Replacements

While Mather works on security, other scientists are working on robots that can take the place of human limbs. In the early 2000s, Yoky Matsuoka created a robotic hand and arm. Her goal is to make something that is as close to a human hand and arm as possible and can be controlled by the wearer's brain.

To create a lifelike limb, Matsuoka mimics the actual structure of a human arm. Her model is made with bone-shaped pieces forming a skeleton. Instead of human muscles and tendons, her model has threads and 30 motors that control movements, including bending and grasping.[4]

The hand-to-brain connection may be many years in the making. First, Matsuoka and her team have to understand how brain signals work and how the muscles and tendons receive those signals. In a process known as neurobotics, the brain commands will have to travel from human muscle to wires leading into the hand.

Matsuoka's robotic hand will take years to perfect, but it is a life-changing invention.

Cooperative Coding

As with Matsuoka, people who work in robotics and computers often work in teams. One of the first things Tracy Chou did when she started working at Pinterest in 2011 was to build a codebase refactor. A refactor simplifies the code that tells the computer what to do without changing how the code works or how things look. In refactoring, small changes are made so it is less likely that a problem will occur than if large changes were made.

Because of Chou's codebase refactor, the multiple programmers in Pinterest's design team could all contribute to the coding on a single project. Refactoring kept their code lines simple and working together.

Perhaps even more important is Chou's work on behalf of other women who want to work with computers. Chou's first class in computer science was so intimidating she temporarily changed her major to avoid having to take any more computer classes. One of the ways she tries to affect the decisions women and girls are making about studying computing is by being a visible public figure. She also participates each year in the Grace Hopper Celebration of Women in Computing, an annual gathering of female computer technologists.

Hunting Smugglers

Not all scientists want their work in computing to be highly visible. Some, such as Sampriti Bhattacharyya, want their creations to sneak in undetected. Bhattacharyya, a graduate student at MIT, created a football-sized submersible robot that can be used to seek out drug smugglers. The robot made its debut at the International Conference on Intelligent Robots and Systems in September 2014. One side of the robot is flattened to slide along the hull of a ship, scanning it for hollow compartments where smugglers hide drugs and other contraband.

Bhattacharyya invented her robot to scan for cracks in nuclear reactors' water tanks but realized it would be ideal for port security. It is small and propels itself without leaving a visible wake. This means numerous robots could easily check the ships moving in and out of a port. Smugglers would never know the scans were taking place and would lose any opportunity to drop or destroy illegal cargo.

Chou tries to be a visible female figure in the computer programming world, so younger girls have someone to look up to.

Grace Hopper Celebration
of Women in Computing

The annual Grace Hopper Celebration of Women in Computing conference is the largest gathering of females working or interested in the technology industry. This event gives thousands of scientists a chance to network during a career fair. Women work on proposals and mentor each other, with more experienced technicians encouraging and guiding younger scientists. A variety of speakers share their experience and advice.

The celebration began in 1994 in honor of Grace Murray Hopper. It has been held in Houston, Texas, multiple times. The event became so popular in the United States that one of the sponsoring organizations, the Anita Borg Institute, started a similar celebration in India each year.

Speakers at the 2015 event included Manuela M. Veloso from Carnegie Mellon University, who specializes in robotics and artificial intelligence, and Miral Kotb, whose work at iLuminate combines technology and dance onstage. The conference also featured Megan Smith, who serves as US chief technology officer in the Office of Science and Technology. In this role, she assists the US president on matters of technology policy and data. Scientists attend this event to learn about the latest developments, to pass on knowledge to others, and to get to know other computer scientists whose interests and passions are similar to their own.

Women in India take part in a coding event as part of the Grace Hopper Celebration of Women in Computing.

In 2012, Bhattacharyya founded the Lab-X Foundation to encourage girls to build, break, and rebuild things. "It's never too late to start building . . . if you really want it," she says.[5]

Digital Security

When Mather founded Silver Tail Systems, companies did not understand the importance of digital security. Now banking, communications, and education often take place digitally. Because of all of this online commerce, cybercrime gangs fight to gain online access to credit cards, bank accounts, and more. They have managed to access approximately 40 percent of the world's 800 million Internet-connected computers.[6] They do this by using viruses and other hacks to corrupt background applications such as Java and Flash, which people use online every day.

Fortunately, scientists such as Window Snyder are working to stop them. At Microsoft, Snyder worked on security for Windows. When she later worked for Mozilla, she secured the company's browser, Firefox.

Now Snyder works for Fastly, a company that provides web services for businesses. Snyder makes sure their clients keep customer information secure by rapidly identifying and avoiding any threats. Scientists such as Snyder work to keep our information safe in an increasingly digital world.

As more companies rely on the Internet,
the work of scientists like Snyder becomes
increasingly important to stop viruses and hacks.

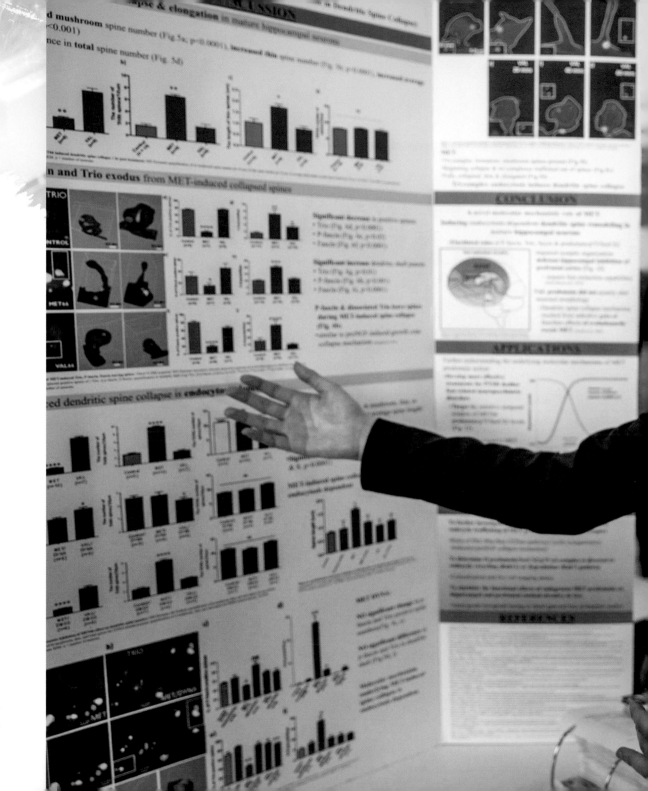

A finalist at the Intel Science Talent Search explains her project.

CHAPTER NINE

Young Scientists Not Waiting until Tomorrow

Today, young women worldwide are using science to solve problems in their communities. In addition to science fairs held in their high schools and communities, they compete in the Intel Science Talent Search and the Google Science Fair.

The Intel Science Talent Search is open to US high school seniors. Online applications are judged on scientific merit, aptitude, and the student's potential as a future leader in the scientific community. Forty finalists travel to Washington, DC, and present their research at the Intel Science Talent Institute. From these 40 students, nine finalists share prizes ranging from $7,500 to $150,000.[1]

(180 metric tons) of banana peels are discarded each day.[4] Throughout high school, she worked on this project. Ten times she created plastics that were not strong enough or decayed too easily. Finally, working with starch from banana peels, Elif made usable plastic. To be sure she had succeeded, she did it a second time. Her effort in creating a banana bioplastic earned her the 2013 Science in Action Award from the Google Science Fair.

In addition to pollution, another global problem is disease. Sixteen-year-old Olivia Hallisey of the United States saw how hard it can be to test for Ebola. The current test must be continually refrigerated and takes up to 12 hours to yield results. This is a problem for communities that may not have reliable electricity and need results quickly to avoid a health crisis. Olivia's test is stored at room temperature, is water activated, and yields results in 30 minutes, even if the person is not showing symptoms.[5] Olivia won the 2015 Google Science Fair Grand Prize for her project.

Other young scientists take on issues that affect the health of the entire planet. When 16-year-old Laura Steponavičiūtė of Lithuania was reading about nanotechnologies, she wanted to know if nanotechnologies released into the environment could be a potential problem. She conducted an experiment to see how nanotechnologies might influence plant growth and discovered a negative effect on the growth of algae. Laura was a Google Science Fair 2015 finalist for her project.

Young scientists work in every area, including genetics. Seventeen-year-old Mimi Yen investigated the mating behavior of *C. elegans*, a microscopic worm. Because the *C. elegans*

Jobs in *Science*

Students interested in and educated in science will be the problem solvers of tomorrow. What types of jobs will be open to them? This graph shows the areas in which experts expect the number of science jobs to increase. Many of these jobs will be in computers and medicine. Women and girls who study math and science will have an opportunity to fill these jobs.[9]

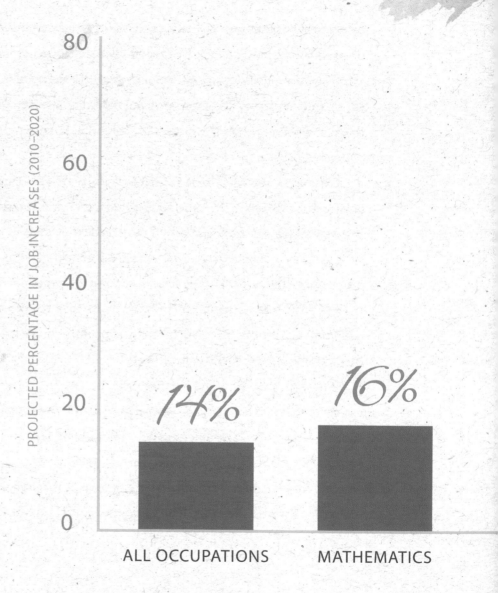

PROJECTED PERCENTAGE IN JOB INCREASES (2010–2020)

80

60

40

20

0

14%

16%

ALL OCCUPATIONS   MATHEMATICS

Projected Percentage Increases in STEM Jobs: 2010–2020

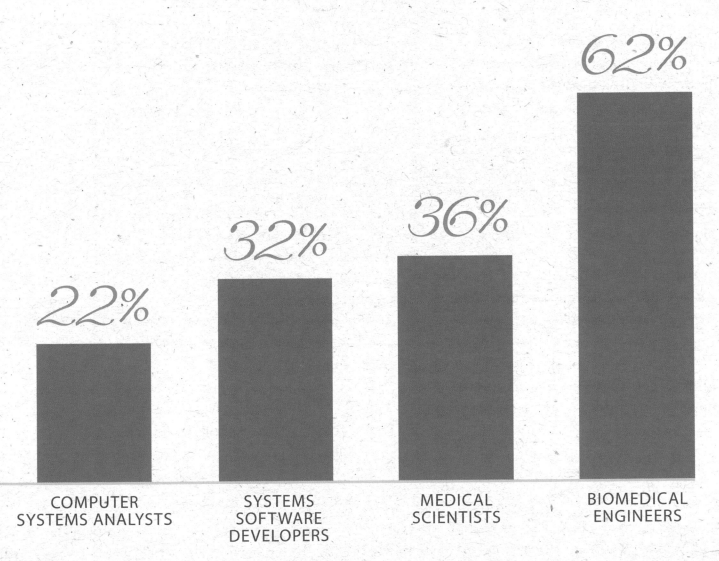

Additional Resources

SELECTED BIBLIOGRAPHY

Schiebinger, Londa. "Women in Science: Historical Perspectives." *Proceedings of the Women in Astronomy Workshop*. Baltimore: Space Telescope Science Institute, 1992. Web. 9 Dec. 2015.

Swaby, Rachel. *Headstrong: 52 Women Who Changed Science—and the World*. New York: Broadway, 2015. Print.

Yount, Lisa. *A to Z of Women in Science and Math*. New York: Facts on File, 2008. Print.

FURTHER READINGS

Coleman, Miriam. *Women in Science*. New York: PowerKids, 2016. Print.

Conkling, Winifred. *Radioactive!: How Irene Curie and Lise Meitner Revolutionized Science and Changed the World*. Chapel Hill, NC: Algonquin Young Readers, 2016. Print.

Krieg, Katherine. *Marie Curie: Physics and Chemistry Pioneer*. Minneapolis, MN: Abdo, 2015. Print.

Macy, Sue. *Sally Ride: Life on a Mission*. New York: Aladdin, 2014. Print.

WEBSITES

To learn more about Women's Lives in History, visit **booklinks.abdopublishing.com**. These links are routinely monitored and updated to provide the most current information available.

FOR MORE INFORMATION

For more information on this subject, contact or visit the following organizations:

Girls in Science, Burke Museum of Natural History and Culture
University of Washington
17th Avenue NE and NE 45th Street
Seattle, WA 98105
206-543-5591
http://www.burkemuseum.org/education/girls_in_science
Saturday and summer study programs inspire girls in the Seattle area to take an interest in science.

Women in Natural Sciences (WINS), Drexel University
1900 Benjamin Franklin Parkway
Philadelphia, PA 19103
215-299-1064
http://www.ansp.org/education/programs/wins/
This free after-school and summer enrichment program is open to eighth-grade girls living in the Philadelphia area.

Women in Science, The Field Museum
1400 South Lake Shore Drive
Chicago, IL 60605
312-922-9410
https://www.fieldmuseum.org/about/employee-groups/women-science
This group devotes its time to promoting an interest in and study of science among women and girls. Look here for information, support, and programming.

Source Notes Continued

2. Ibid.

3. Kathy A. Svitil. "The 50 Most Important Women in Science." *Discover.* Kalmbach Publishing, 1 Nov. 2002. Web. 23 Dec. 2015.

CHAPTER 6. WOMEN AND SPACE

1. Corey S. Powell. "Sara Seager's Tenacious Drive to Discover Another Earth." *Smithsonian.com.* Smithsonian.com, May 2014. Web. 23 Dec. 2015.

2. Ibid.

3. Ibid.

4. Jeffrey Hoffman. "Sally Kristen Ride." *Physics Today.* Physics Today, February 2013: 62. Web. 23 Dec. 2015.

5. Ibid.

6. "First Woman in Space." *History.* A&E Television Networks, n.d. Web. 23 Dec. 2015.

7. Charles Q. Choi. "Strange 'Hybrid Star' Discovered After 40-Year Search." *Space.com.* Space.com, 9 Oct. 2014. Web. 23 Dec. 2015.

8. Emmie Martin. "The 15 Most Amazing Women in Science Today." *MSN.* Microsoft, 16 July 2015. Web. 23 Dec. 2015.

9. Biography.com Editors. "Ellen Ochoa Biography." *Biography.com.* A&E Television Networks, n.d. Web. 23 Dec. 2015.

CHAPTER 7. WOMEN IN MATHEMATICS AND ENGINEERING

1. Amanda Siegfried. "Professor Plots Course for Sun-Studying Spacecraft." *Purdue News.* Purdue News, 1998. Web. 23 Dec. 2015.

2. "Her Story Then and Now, Lillian Moller Gilbreth." *Women in Science, Technology, Engineering and Mathematics.* WAMC Northeast Public Radio, n.d. Web. 23 Dec. 2015.

3. "Maria Chudnovsky." *MacArthur Foundation.* John D. and Catherine T. MacArthur Foundation, 2 Oct. 2012. Web. 23 Dec. 2015.

4. JR Minkel. "Maria Chudnovsky." *Popular Science.* Popular Science, 29 June 2004. Web. 23 Dec. 2015.

5. "Interview with Research Fellow Maria Chudnovsky." *CMI Annual Report.* CMI, n.d. Web. 23 Dec. 2015.

6. Rachel Swaby. *Headstrong: 52 Women who Changed Science—and the World.* New York: Broadway, 2015. Print.

7. "Milestones: Harvard Mark I Computer, 1944–1959." *Engineering and Technology History Wiki.* ETHW, 9 July 2015. Web. 23 Dec. 2015.

CHAPTER 8. WOMEN IN COMPUTING AND ROBOTICS

1. James Temple. "Boston Researcher Cynthia Breazeal is Ready to Bring Robots Into the Home. Are You?" *Recode*. Vox Media, n.d. Web. 23 Dec. 2015.

2. Rachel Swaby. *Headstrong: 52 Women who Changed Science—and the World*. New York: Broadway, 2015. Print.182–185.

3. "Laura Mather." LinkedIn.com. LinkedIn, n.d. Web. 23 Dec. 2015.

4. "Bionic Woman." *NOVA*. WGBH Educational Foundation, 1 July 2008. Web. 23 Dec. 2015.

5. Michelle Millier. "Female Roboticist Wants Girls to Build, Break, and Make Things." *Product Lifecycle Report*. PTC, 21 Nov. 2014. Web. 23 Dec. 2015.

6. Ibid.

CHAPTER 9. YOUNG SCIENTISTS NOT WAITING UNTIL TOMORROW

1. "Judging and Awards." *Student Science*. Society for Science and the Public, n.d. Web. 23 Dec. 2015.

2. "Prizes." *Google Science Fair*. The LEGO Group, n.d. Web. 23 Dec. 2015.

3. "Mission and Vision." *Girls Who Code*. Girls Who Code, 2015. Web. 23 Dec. 2015.

4. Amanda Froelich. "She Invented Bio-Plastic from Banana Peels when She Was Just 16 Years Old." *True Activist*. True Activist, 12 Sept. 2013. Web. 23 Dec. 2015.

5. "Olivia Hallisey." *Google Science Fair*. The LEGO Group, n.d. Web. 23 Dec. 2015.

6. "NYC-Area High School Student Working with NYU Biologists Captures Third Place at INTEL Science Talent Search." *New York University*. New York University, 19 Mar. 2012. Web. 23 Dec. 2015.

7. Stephen J. Ceci, Donna Ginther, Shulamit Kahn, Wendy Williams. "Women in Science: The Path to Progress." *Scientific American Mind*. Scientific American Mind, Jan./Feb. 2015: 62–69. Web. 23 Dec. 2015.

8. Ibid.

9. "Science, Technology, Engineering and Math: Education for Global Leadership." *US Department of Education*. US Department of Education, n.d. Web. 23 Dec. 2015.

Index

About the Author

Sue Bradford Edwards writes nonfiction for children and teens, working from her home in Saint Louis, Missouri. Unlike many girls, Edwards was never discouraged from taking classes in science or mathematics. When she went to college, she studied anthropology, and had classes in paleoanthropology, biology, microbiology, and chemistry. Her books for young readers covers a wide range of topics including *Ancient Maya*, *The Bombing of Pearl Harbor*, *Black Lives Matter*, *Gertrude Ederle versus the English Channel*, and *12 Incredible Facts about the Cuban Missile Crisis*.